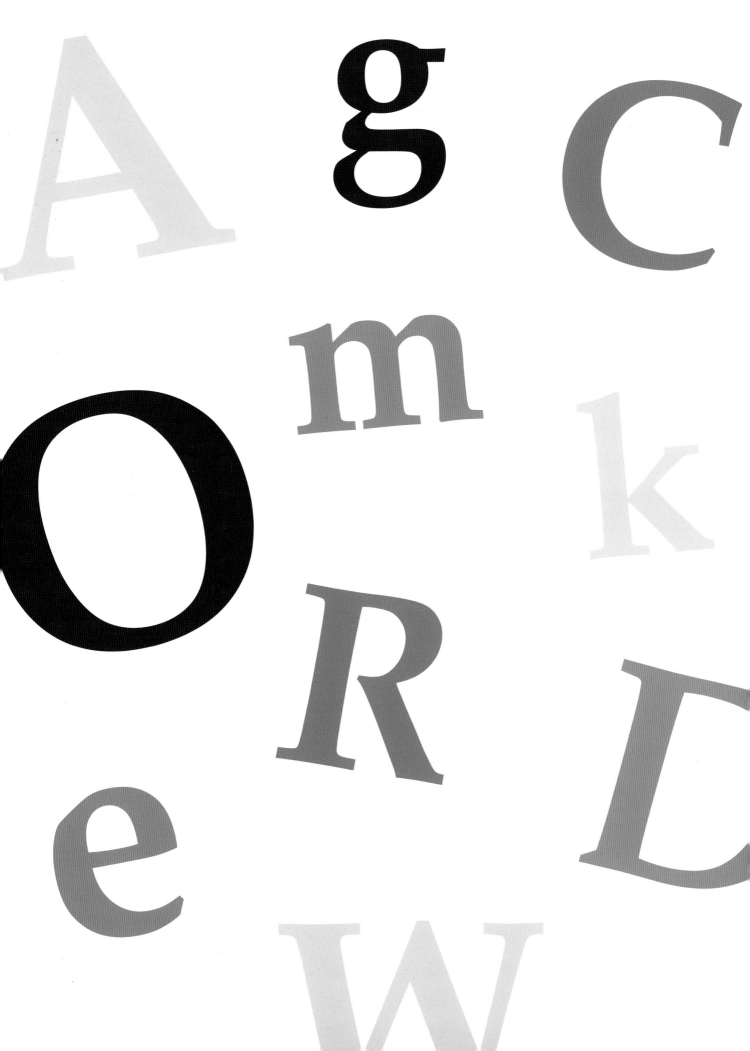

Published by Creative Education
123 South Broad Street, Mankato, Minnesota 56001

Creative Education is an imprint of The Creative Company.
Design by Stephanie Blumenthal
Production design by The Design Lab
Art direction by Rita Marshall

Photographs by Corbis (Academy of Natural Sciences of Philadelphia, Archivo Iconografico, S.A., Bettmann, Horace Bristol, David Butow, Contemporary African Art Collection Limited, Pat Doyle, Paul Gun, Cynthia Hart Designer, Francis G. Mayer, North Carolina Museum of Art, Scheufler Collection)

"Poem (As the cat)" by William Carlos Williams, from *Collected Poems: 1909-1939, Volume I*, copyright © 1938 by New Directions Publishing Corp. Reprinted by permission of New Directions Publishing Corp. / "anyone lived in a pretty how town". Copyright 1940, © 1968, 1991 by the Trustees for the E. E. Cummings Trust, from *Complete Poems: 1904-1962* by E. E. Cummings, edited by George J. Firmage. Used by permission of Liveright Publishing Corporation. / "Theme for English B" from *The Collected Poems of Langston Hughes* by Langston Hughes, copyright © 1994 by The Estate of Langston Hughes. Used by permission of Alfred A. Knopf, a division of Random House, Inc. / "The Bean Eaters" from *Blacks* by Gwendolyn Brooks. Reprinted By Consent of Brooks Permissions. / "The Truth the Dead Know" from *All My Pretty Ones* by Anne Sexton. Copyright © 1962 by Anne Sexton, renewed 1990 by Linda G. Sexton. Reprinted by permission of Houghton Mifflin Company. All rights reserved. / All lines from "Morning Song" from *Ariel* by Sylvia Plath. Copyright © 1961 by Ted Hughes. Reprinted by permission of HarperCollins Publishers Inc. / "Introduction to Poetry" from *The Apple That Astonished Paris* by Billy Collins. Reprinted by permission of the University of Arkansas Press. Copyright 1988 by Billy Collins. / "Digging" from *Opened Ground: Selected Poems 1966-1996* by Seamus Heaney. Copyright © 1998 by Seamus Heaney. Reprinted by permission of Farrar, Straus and Giroux, LLC.

Library of Congress Cataloging-in-Publication Data

Fandel, Jennifer.
Keats, Shakespeare, and other wordsmiths / by Jennifer Fandel.
p. cm. — (Understanding poetry)
Includes bibliographical references and index.
ISBN 1-58341-343-X
1. English poetry—History and criticism—Juvenile literature. 2. American poetry—History and criticism—Juvenile literature. I. Title.

PR502.F36 2004
821.009—dc22   2004058224

First edition

2 4 6 8 9 7 5 3 1

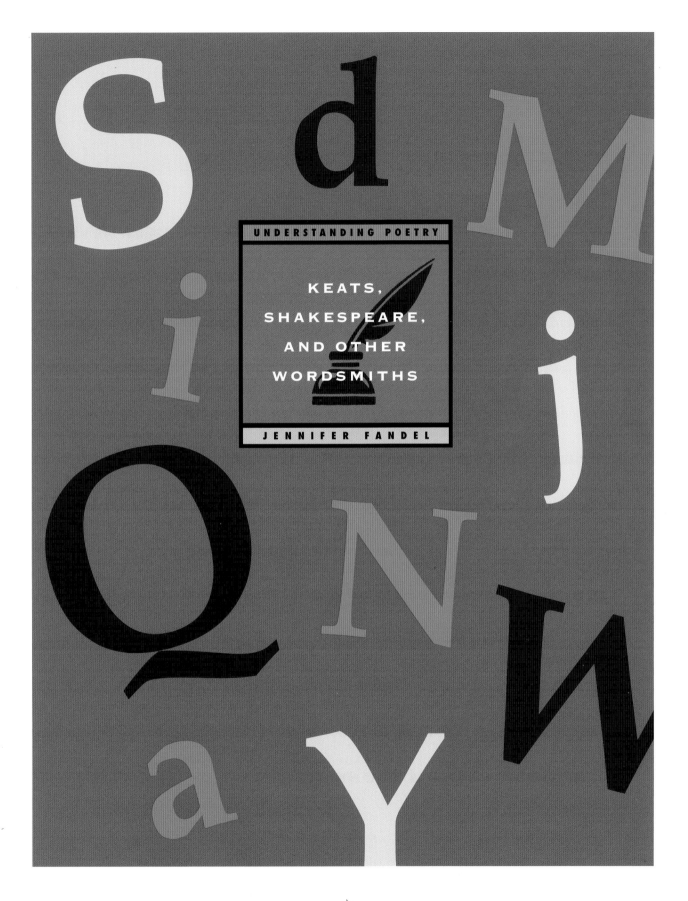

UNDERSTANDING POETRY

KEATS,
SHAKESPEARE,
AND OTHER
WORDSMITHS

JENNIFER FANDEL

CREATIVE EDUCATION

SHAKESPEARE & KEATS

To-morrow, and to-morrow, and to-morrow,
Creeps in this petty pace from day to day,
To the last syllable of recorded time;
And all our yesterdays have lighted fools
The way to dusty death. Out, out, brief candle!
Life's but a walking shadow, a poor player,
That struts and frets his hour upon the stage,
And then is heard no more. It is a tale
Told by an idiot, full of sound and fury,
Signifying nothing.

from *Macbeth*, act 5, scene 5
— by William Shakespeare

In John Keats's famous poem "Ode on a Grecian Urn,"

he writes, "'Beauty is truth, truth beauty'—that is all /

Ye know on earth, and all ye need to know." This often-quoted line helps reveal the com-

mon threads between the English poets William Shakespeare (1564–1616) and John Keats

(1795–1821), even though they wrote nearly 200 years apart. Both poets illuminated the

complex thoughts and emotions of human life. Carefully

observing humans and nature, they found beauty in the ordinary life around them.

William Shakespeare was born in 1564 in Stratford-upon-Avon to a merchant-class family. He attended school until age 12 or 13, at which time he began his apprenticeship in his father's glove-making business. At age 18, he married a local woman and eventually had three children with her. By the age of 28, Shakespeare's plays were drawing the attention of critics and theater-goers alike. While best known for his 37 plays, Shakespeare also wrote 154 **sonnets** and 2 **narrative poems**—all within a span of 30 years. He died in 1616 at the age of 52.

Many people think of Shakespeare's plays as something separate from his poetry, but the playwright used poetry to compose his plays. Shakespeare's plays are written in **blank verse**, a special type of meter, and filled with poetic language. In addition, he invented a new type of sonnet, called the Shakespearean sonnet, which used a different type of **rhyme scheme** from other sonnets before it.

Shakespeare's ability with meter, rhyme, and word choice is much admired, but it is the humanity of his works for which he's best remembered. His words continue to make readers laugh, weep, ache, and rejoice. In Shakespeare, readers hear their own voices, their own thoughts, and their own dreams.

John Keats was born in 1795 outside London. After losing his father to an accident at the age of 8, and his mother to tuberculosis at 14, Keats shouldered the responsibility for his three younger siblings. His concern and love for them helped the family stay close long after their childhood. Additionally, relatives made sure that the children received a good education. At the age of 15, Keats was apprenticed to an apothecary, or pharmacist. Six years later, he received his license to practice medicine on his own. However, Keats's heart belonged to poetry.

A year after giving up his work in medicine, Keats published his first volume of poetry. He threw himself into the literary scene, making friends with William Wordsworth and Percy Bysshe Shelley, leading poets in the **Romantic Movement**. He produced an amazing number of poems in 1818 and 1819, despite joys and setbacks. During this time, Keats fell in love and became engaged. But soon after, one of his brothers died of tuberculosis, leaving Keats to deal with his family's financial problems. Unfortunately, Keats also developed a severe sore throat that slowly progressed into a painful illness. Hoping that mild weather would cure him, he moved to Italy in 1820. In 1821, he died of tuberculosis at the young age of 25.

Keats saw poetry as a way to imaginatively capture the world and make it new for his readers. Even though he spent only 5 of his 25 years fulfilling his dream of being a poet, his legacy reminds us to appreciate beauty on Earth.

ON THE GRASSHOPPER AND THE CRICKET

The poetry of earth is never dead:

When all the birds are faint with the hot sun,

And hide in cooling trees, a voice will run

From hedge to hedge about the new-mown mead;

That is the Grasshopper's—he takes the lead

In summer luxury,—he has never done

With his delights; for when tired out with fun

He rests at ease beneath some pleasant weed.

The poetry of earth is ceasing never:

On a long winter evening, when the frost

Has wrought a silence, from the stove there shrills

The Cricket's song, in warmth increasing ever,

And seems to one in drowsiness half lost,

The Grasshopper's among some grassy hills.

— by John Keats

I celebrate myself, and sing myself,

And what I assume you shall assume,

For every atom belonging to me as good belongs to you.

I loafe and invite my soul,

I lean and loafe at my ease observing a spear of summer grass.

My tongue, every atom of my blood, form'd from this soil, this air,

Born here of parents born here from parents the same, and their parents the same,

I, now thirty-seven years old in perfect health begin,

Hoping to cease not till death.

Creeds and schools in abeyance,

Retiring back a while sufficed at what they are, but never forgotten,

I harbor for good or bad, I permit to speak at every hazard,

Nature without check with original energy.

from *Song of Myself*

— by Walt Whitman

11

American poets Walt Whitman (1819–92) and Emily Dickinson (1830–86) led dramatically different lives, but together their poems transformed American poetry. During the 1800s, at a time when poets often looked to Europe for artistic inspiration, Whitman and Dickinson found inspiration in the ordinary life around them. Compared to popular poems of that time, their poems were rough and untamed, breaking away from traditional meters and rhymes. At a time when much poetry focused on public subjects (such as nature), influential people, and important events in history, Whitman and Dickinson celebrated their personal visions and private lives. Their poems shattered people's ideas about poetry and inspired generations of poets to come.

Walt Whitman was born in 1819 and grew up in Brooklyn, New York. As the second of nine children in a working-class family, Whitman attended school for only five years before learning the printer's trade. An adventurous man, Whitman also worked as a

teacher, a journalist, and a nurse in army hospitals during the Civil War. Through all of his adventures, he considered poetry his life's work.

Whitman began his publishing career at age 22. At the time, he wrote in strict meter and rhyme, the typical style of poetry in those days. He also acted as he thought a poet should, wearing fashionable clothes and using his given name, "Walter." However, that changed when Whitman read the call from Ralph Waldo Emerson, an influential writer and philosopher, for a poet to celebrate the distinct culture and voice of America. Whitman's response to this call was the 1855 book *Leaves of Grass*. Whitman's picture graced the book's cover. Gone was the fashionable New Yorker known as Walter. He had transformed into a long-bearded man in rough workman's clothes who went by the name "Walt."

No one had seen poetry like his before. It was written in a casual voice, as if the poet were speaking personally to his audience. The subject matter was simple and earthy. And the lines were long and seemingly unstructured, sprawling across each page. He died in 1892, and since that time, his free verse style has inspired poets to experiment with different styles and forms. His voice, the voice of the common man, made American poetry something different, something individual.

Emily Dickinson was born in 1830 in Amherst, Massachusetts. She grew up with a brother and sister in a well-established family, as her father was a prominent lawyer and member of Congress. An inquisitive and well-educated woman, Dickinson left home at age 17 to continue her education at Mount Holyoke Female Seminary. The school was not far from home, but Dickinson quit in less than a year because of severe homesickness. Although Dickinson liked the familiarity of home, she was believed to be quite sociable in her early years. However, an unknown emotional tragedy in her life sent her into hiding. By the age of 30, Dickinson was a recluse, a loner who seldom saw visitors and dressed completely in white.

Poetry was important to Dickinson from an early age. She wrote poems whenever thoughts and images occurred to her, often writing on the backs of receipts, envelopes, and grocery bags. By the end of her life, she had written about 1,800 poems. But she had little interest in publication, and only 10 of her poems were published when she was alive. After Dickinson's death in 1886, her sister asked friends of the family to collect and edit the poems for publication. In 1890, Dickinson's first book was published, stunning the world with her playful language, unusual punctuation, and striking imagery.

Dickinson's poems were often serious and bold, focusing on her personal life and emotions. And her work showed future generations of poets that great subject matter was all around them; they needed only to examine their lives to find it.

16

986

A narrow Fellow in the Grass
Occasionally rides—
You may have met Him—did you not
His notice sudden is—

The Grass divides as with a Comb—
A spotted shaft is seen—
And then it closes at your feet
And opens further on—

He likes a Boggy Acre
A Floor too cool for Corn—
Yet when a Boy, and Barefoot—
I more than once at Noon
Have passed, I thought, a Whip lash
Unbraiding in the Sun
When stooping to secure it
It wrinkled, and was gone—

Several of Nature's People
I know, and they know me—
I feel for them a transport
Of cordiality—

But never met this Fellow
Attended, or alone
Without a tighter breathing
And Zero at the Bone—

— by Emily Dickinson

17

POEM

As the cat
climbed over
the top of

the jamcloset
first the right
forefoot

carefully
then the hind
stepped down

into the pit of
the empty
flowerpot

— by William Carlos Williams

In the early 1900s, two distinct voices emerged out of the many new artistic movements and styles developing at the time. American poets William Carlos Williams (1883–1963) and E. E. Cummings (1894–1962) offered readers an alternative to the complex poetry being written by T. S. Eliot and Ezra Pound, two American poets who lived in Europe and found their inspiration there. Like Whitman and Dickinson in the century before, both Williams and Cummings offered simplicity in their styles, with accessible word choices, exact images, and emphasis on spoken language. In many ways, Williams and Cummings pushed the transformations in American poetry further through their experiments with form, language, subject matter, and imagery.

William Carlos Williams, born in 1883 in Rutherford, New Jersey, was well-educated and grew up admiring art and literature, just as his parents did. Despite their love of the arts and their son's early experiments with poetry in high school, they encouraged Williams to pursue medicine. He attended the University of Pennsylvania's medical program, where he met Ezra Pound and other poets who encouraged his writing. His first volume of poetry was published when he was only 20 years old. After graduating from the university, he opened his own private medical practice and worked as a doctor for the next 40 years. During that time, he continued to write and publish poetry, stories, novels, essays, and an autobiography. He died in 1963, shortly after receiving the Pulitzer Prize for his poetry collection *Pictures from Breugel and Other Poems*.

Like Whitman, Williams wanted a poetry that represented America, and he believed he could accomplish that by using the everyday images and language of average Americans. In his early years, Williams was one of the leaders of the **Imagist** Movement begun by Pound. However, Williams grew tired of the focus on Europe and split away from the group. The ideas of the imagist movement, though, were something that Williams fully believed in. His famous line "No ideas but in things" summarized his belief in images to make scenes and moments come alive.

E. E. (Edward Estlin) Cummings, the son of a Unitarian minister, was born in 1894 in Cambridge, Massachusetts. A bright and motivated student, Cummings attended Harvard University, receiving his bachelor's and master's degree in English and Classics by the time he was 22 years old. He then worked odd jobs for a year before volunteering for the French ambulance service during World War I. After his war service, Cummings moved to Paris to study visual art and writing, and he traveled between Paris and New York while working as a writer for *Vanity Fair* magazine in the 1920s.

In 1923, Cummings's first book of poetry, *Tulips and Chimneys*, was published. Inspired by the art world, especially jazz music and the fragmented images seen in **Cubist** paintings of the time, Cummings was interested in the look of words on the page. He experimented with punctuation and capitalization, and used words in offbeat ways, changing their order in a sentence, breaking them into syllables, or inventing new ones. Some people thought his poetry was complex, but Cummings believed his experiments with language simplified things, bringing people to a truer, more real understanding of the world around them.

Cummings devoted his life to being a writer and artist. He tried to see as a child and to rediscover language. Since his death in 1962, Cummings's poetry has continued to show readers the joys of language and the emotions that live inside each word.

anyone lived in a pretty how town

anyone lived in a pretty how town
(with up so floating many bells down)
spring summer autumn winter
he sang his didn't he danced his did.

Women and men(both little and small)
cared for anyone not at all
they sowed their isn't they reaped their same
sun moon stars rain

children guessed(but only a few
and down they forgot as up they grew
autumn winter spring summer)
that noone loved him more by more

when by now and tree by leaf
she laughed his joy she cried his grief
bird by snow and stir by still
anyone's any was all to her

someones married their everyones
laughed their cryings and did their dance
(sleep wake hope and then)they
said their nevers they slept their dream

stars rain sun moon
(and only the snow can begin to explain
how children are apt to forget to remember
with up so floating many bells down)

one day anyone died i guess
(and noone stooped to kiss his face)
busy folk buried them side by side
little by little and was by was

all by all and deep by deep
and more by more they dream their sleep
noone and anyone earth by april
wish by spirit and if by yes.

Women and men(both dong and ding)
summer autumn winter spring
reaped their sowing and went their came
sun moon stars rain

— by E. E. Cummings

23

THEME FOR ENGLISH B

The instructor said,

Go home and write

a page tonight.

And let that page come out of you—

Then, it will be true.

I wonder if it's that simple?

I am twenty-two, colored, born in Winston-Salem.

I went to school there, then Durham, then here

to this college on the hill above Harlem.

I am the only colored student in my class.

The steps from the hill lead down into Harlem,

through a park, then I cross St. Nicholas,

Eighth Avenue, Seventh, and I come to the Y,

the Harlem Branch Y, where I take the elevator

up to my room, sit down, and write this page:

It's not easy to know what is true for you or me

at twenty-two, my age. But I guess I'm what

I feel and see and hear, Harlem, I hear you:

hear you, hear me—we two—you, me, talk on

   this page.

(I hear New York, too.) Me—who?

Well, I like to eat, sleep, drink, and be in love.

I like to work, read, learn, and understand life.

I like a pipe for a Christmas present,

or records—Bessie, bop, or Bach.

I guess being colored doesn't make me *not* like

the same things other folks like who are other

   races.

So will my page be colored that I write?

Being me, it will not be white.

But it will be

a part of you, instructor.

You are white—

yet a part of me, as I am a part of you.

That's American.

Sometimes perhaps you don't want to be a

   part of me.

Nor do I often want to be a part of you.

But we are, that's true!

As I learn from you,

I guess you learn from me—

although you're older—and white—

and somewhat more free.

This is my page for English B.

— by Langston Hughes

African-American poets Langston Hughes (1902–67) and Gwendolyn Brooks (1917–2000) brought black poetry, and poetry of other minorities, to the forefront of American literature. Langston Hughes was the leading figure of the **Harlem Renaissance**. Gwendolyn Brooks, inspired by Hughes's work, picked up where he left off. Both Hughes and Brooks gave minorities a face, a name, and a voice, and readers today continue to look to their poems for their music, images, and great humanity.

Langston Hughes was born in 1902 in Joplin, Missouri. Soon after his birth, his parents separated, and Langston spent his early years living with his grandmother. In elementary school, fellow students voted him class poet, an honor that he took to heart. After high school, Langston studied engineering, at his father's request, at Columbia University. After one year, Langston dropped out to pursue writing. In that same year, his poem "A Negro Speaks of Rivers" was published in a leading African-American magazine. He worked odd jobs, traveling to the west coast of Africa, the Soviet Union, Rotterdam, and Paris, and eventually settled in Harlem, New York.

His name soon became known in local literary circles, and his first book of poems, *The Weary Blues*, was published in 1926. In the 1930s, he became the first African-American to make his living solely as a writer and lecturer. The 1940s were his most productive time; he wrote novels, short stories, plays, essays, and poetry. His most important and most popular book, *Montage of a Dream Deferred*, was published in 1951.

Hughes was the first poet to incorporate the rhythm and language of black music, namely blues and jazz, into poetry. He was also one of the first black poets to incorporate the **slang** and **colloquialisms** of black language. He drew from the **oral tradition** of the black working class, and he focused on the plight of poor blacks who dreamed of freedom and opportunity. Like Williams and Cummings, who were both writing at this time, Hughes was trying to expand views of what poetry was.

Gwendolyn Brooks was born in 1917 in Topeka, Kansas, but she lived the rest of her life in Chicago, Illinois. A shy, thoughtful girl who loved to read, Brooks excelled in school. Education and reading were highly prized in her home, and she fell in love with the poems that her parents recited and encouraged her to learn. At age 13, Brooks had her first poem published. In high school, she had the privilege of meeting Langston Hughes, who encouraged her literary ambitions. After graduating from high school, Brooks attended college and became a staff writer for a leading African-American newspaper with her own regular poetry column. In 1939, she married writer and poet Henry Blakely, and they had two children.

Recognition for Brooks's poetry began arriving in the 1940s. Her first book of poems, *A Street in Bronzeville*, published in 1945, was admired by both critics and readers. And in 1950, with her second collection of poems, *Annie Allen*, she became the first black poet to receive a Pulitzer Prize. In 1968, she became Poet Laureate of Illinois, a post that she held until her death in 2000. She also served as the poet consultant to the Library of Congress (a position now called the poet laureate of the United States) from 1985 to 1986.

In many of her poems, Brooks tells stories of individual African-Americans living in the inner city and struggling to survive. Influenced heavily by Hughes's work, Brooks tried to capture the essence of black life. Through her language, music, and imagery, she made the beauty and sadness of everyday life sing on the page.

THE BEAN EATERS

They eat beans mostly, this old yellow pair.

Dinner is a casual affair.

Plain chipware on a plain and creaking wood,

Tin flatware.

Two who are Mostly Good.

Two who have lived their day,

But keep on putting on their clothes

And putting things away.

And remembering . . .

Remembering, with twinklings and twinges,

As they lean over the beans in their rented back room that is full of beads and receipts and

    dolls and cloths, tobacco crumbs, vases and fringes.

— by Gwendolyn Brooks

THE TRUTH THE DEAD KNOW

For my mother, born March 1902, died March 1959
and my father, born February 1900, died June 1959

Gone, I say and walk from church,
refusing the stiff procession to the grave,
letting the dead ride alone in the hearse.
It is June. I am tired of being brave.

We drive to the Cape. I cultivate
myself where the sun gutters from the sky,
where the sea swings in like an iron gate
and we touch. In another country people die.

My darling, the wind falls in like stones
from the whitehearted water and when we touch
we enter touch entirely. No one's alone.
Men kill for this, or for as much.

And what of the dead? They lie without shoes
in their stone boats. They are more like stone
than the sea would be if it stopped. They refuse
to be blessed, throat, eye and knucklebone.

— by Anne Sexton

Anne Sexton (1928–74) and Sylvia Plath (1932–63) were both considered part of the "**confessional**" school of poetry, a movement that focused on exploring people's inner lives and emotions. Until the 1950s, women were encouraged to write about public subjects, such as nature. Anything personal was typically disguised through imagery or references to common myths or stories. In their work, Sexton and Plath addressed menstruation, the pains and joys of childbirth, their mental and emotional breakdowns, and the struggles they endured as women. By breaking through these barriers, they showed poets—both women and men—that people's private lives were full of meaning that did not need to be disguised. Both women's untimely deaths due to suicide were a devastating loss to readers and poets alike.

Anne Sexton was born in 1928 in Newton, Massachusetts. She attended prep school and one year of finishing school in Boston before eloping at age 19. In 1953, at age 25, she gave birth to her first daughter. After the birth, Sexton was diagnosed with severe depression and was hospitalized for a mental breakdown. In 1955, after the birth of her second child, this cycle repeated itself. While Sexton was recovering from her second breakdown, her therapist suggested writing to deal with her feelings. Sexton attended workshops to share her poetry, was soon accepted into Boston University's graduate writing program, and published her first book of poems, *To Bedlam and Part Way Back,* in 1960.

After her initial success, Sexton began teaching writing. She continued to publish her poetry and was in high demand for her emotional readings. However, despite her success, her mental problems never went away, and she occasionally tried to commit suicide. In 1974, she succeeded at ending her life.

Sexton's poems changed women's poetry and people's perceptions of women. Filled with raw emotion, her poetry emphasized the differences between women and men, while also showing the world that women were just as complex, intelligent, and powerful as men.

Sylvia Plath was born in 1932 in Jamaica Plain, Massachusetts. Compelled to write from an early age, Plath received her first poetry publication at the age of eight and had another poem published in *Seventeen* magazine while in high school. In 1951, she was awarded a scholarship to Smith College, where she immersed herself in writing poems and short stories, producing more than 400 poems. Throughout her teen years and into adulthood, Plath struggled with depression, and she tried to commit suicide at age 21. After an extended hospital stay, Plath returned to college.

In 1956, after finishing her degree, Plath went to study at Cambridge, England, on a Fulbright Scholarship for two years. There she met Ted Hughes, a young British poet whom she married in 1956. Plath later gave birth to two children, one in 1960 and the other in 1962. Unfortunately, the difficulty of writing and raising children put a strain on the couple's marriage, and they separated. In 1963, Plath's depression again worsened, and she committed suicide at age 30.

Plath was an extremely productive poet, and she died at a time when many people felt her poetry was showing great growth and change. Her poetry explored the bright and haunting moments of her life. Each moment, no matter how beautiful, was tinged with a recognition of the pain of living. But for Plath, presenting the personal was never enough. She believed each moment on the page must be shaped into art, and that art is what she left behind for the world to appreciate.

MORNING SONG

Love set you going like a fat gold watch.
The midwife slapped your footsoles, and your bald cry
Took its place among the elements.

Our voices echo, magnifying your arrival. New statue.
In a drafty museum, your nakedness
Shadows our safety. We stand round blankly as walls.

I'm no more your mother
Than the cloud that distills a mirror to reflect its own slow
Effacement at the wind's hand.

All night your moth-breath
Flickers among the flat pink roses. I wake to listen:
A far sea moves in my ear.

One cry, and I stumble from bed, cow-heavy and floral
In my Victorian nightgown.
Your mouth opens clean as a cat's. The window square

Whitens and swallows its dull stars. And now you try
Your handful of notes;
The clear vowels rise like balloons.

— by Sylvia Plath

INTRODUCTION TO POETRY

I ask them to take a poem
and hold it up to the light
like a color slide

or press an ear against its hive.

I say drop a mouse into a poem
and watch him probe his way out,

or walk inside the poem's room
and feel the walls for a light switch.

I want them to waterski
across the surface of a poem
waving at the author's name on the shore.

But all they want to do
is tie the poem to a chair with rope
and torture a confession out of it.

They begin beating it with a hose
to find out what it really means.

— by Billy Collins

Readers are continually looking for poets who speak to them. Sometimes they find these voices in poetry from long ago, but other times readers look for fresh perspectives and new voices. Today's contemporary poets are probably best characterized by the freedom they have to write about the subjects and in the styles that appeal to them. Because of this, it is nearly impossible to define contemporary poetry. If anything is constant, it is probably the great variety present in contemporary poetry. The poems at the beginning and end of this section, "Introduction to Poetry" by Billy Collins and "Digging" by Seamus Heaney, offer a small taste of this variety.

The subject matter of contemporary poetry is very diverse. Some poets, such as Americans Sharon Olds and Galway Kinnell, write about personal matters, similar to Sexton and Plath before them. Other poets believe that all poetry is both personal and political. These poets write about events they have observed, lived, and read about, hoping to show readers the consequences of certain actions and ways of thinking. Americans Carolyn Forché and Robert Bly are two prominent political poets.

Additionally, many contemporary poets focus on subject matter based on their own race. For example, Lucille Clifton, Rita Dove, Yusef Komunyakaa, and Nikki Giovanni write from their experiences as African-Americans, while Alberto Rios and Gary Soto write from the perspectives of their Mexican-American backgrounds. Because our world is more connected than in the past—through speedy communication and travel—more readers are aware of poets from cultures, backgrounds, and countries different from their own.

Contemporary poets also reveal certain personalities in their poems and present their poems differently. Some poets, such as Billy Collins and Stephen Dunn, use humor and make their personality known in much of their poetry. The poems of Mary Oliver and William Stafford, however, are more introspective and serious in nature. Additionally, some poets are drawn much more to the performance of their poetry than others. Most poets agree that reading their poetry aloud is important, and many of them give readings. However, some poets like to perform their poetry with music, movement, or acting. Amiri Baraka is just one of the many poets who has moved away from a traditional podium for her readings, instead using musical accompaniment on a stage to ehance her poems' effect.

Through times of happiness and sorrow, poets wrestle with their own thoughts and struggle to make sense of the world around them. Often, people are not aware of the need for poetry in today's world until something bad happens. After the events of September 11, 2001, when terrorists attacked the United States, many people turned to poetry to help them understand their own questions and feelings. In times of difficulty, we often search for a friend or a consoling word, and sometimes both of these things can be found in poetry.

Poets of past generations, the present generation, and generations yet to come know that we need poetry in our lives. Poems comfort and encourage us. They help us understand ourselves and those around us. And they make our own place in this large world seem a little less small.

DIGGING

Between my finger and my thumb
The squat pen rests; snug as a gun.

Under my window, a clean rasping sound
When the spade sinks into gravelly ground:
My father, digging. I look down

Till his straining rump among the flowerbeds
Bends low, comes up twenty years away
Stooping in rhythm through potato drills
Where he was digging.

The coarse boot nestled on the lug, the shaft
Against the inside knee was levered firmly.
He rooted out tall tops, buried the bright edge deep
To scatter new potatoes that we picked,
Loving their cool hardness
    in our hands.

By god, the old man could handle a spade.
Just like his old man.

My grandfather cut more turf in a day
Than any other man on Toner's bog.
Once I carried him milk in a bottle
Corked sloppily with paper. He straightened up
To drink it, then fell to right away
Nicking and slicing neatly, heaving sods
Over his shoulder, going down and down
For the good turf. Digging.

The cold smell of potato mould, the squelch
   and slap
Of soggy peat, the curt cuts of an edge
Through living roots awaken in my head.
But I've no spade to follow men like them.

Between my finger and my thumb
The squat pen rests.
I'll dig with it.

— by Seamus Heaney

STANZA BREAKS

1. **Recommended Resources: Listening to poets.** The Academy of American Poets Web site (http://www.poets.org) presents biographies of American poets, a selection of their poems, and some audio clips of the poets reading their work. Additionally, the "Lannan Series" and "Poets in Person" are two video series that present contemporary poets reading their poetry and talking about their struggles and joys as writers.

2. **For More Information: Poet laureates.** The poet laureate of the United States is appointed to a one-year position by the Library of Congress. In the position, poets develop a project or focus on a concern of importance to them. To find out more about the position of poet laureate, check out the Library of Congress Web site at http://www.loc.gov/poetry/laureate.html.

3. **Recommended Resources: Web sites.** Two previous poet laureates, Billy Collins and Robert Pinsky, developed poetry Web sites during their time in the position. Billy Collins's project, "Poetry 180," is a poem-a-day collection geared toward high-school students. Robert Pinsky's project, "The Favorite Poem Project," asked Americans to submit some of their favorite poems. These sites can be found at http://www.loc.gov/poetry/180 and http://www.favoritepoem.org.

4. **For More Information: National Poetry Month.** National Poetry Month was started in 1996 and is celebrated every April in the United States. Many schools, libraries, and bookstores hold events to celebrate poetry and make people more aware of the importance of poetry in our daily lives. Look for events in your area or hold your own celebration for National Poetry Month.

5. **Discussion Question: Talk about it.** With a group of friends or classmates, discuss which poets you like best. Why do you like a certain poet's work? What makes his or her work memorable to you? During the

discussion, you'll likely hear a lot of different opinions. The wide variety of subject matter, styles, and voices in poetry mirror and appeal to the wide variety of people in the world.

6. **Activity: Start your own workshop.** Do any of your friends or classmates write poetry? If so, start a workshop! At a workshop, writers share their poems with the group and get feedback to improve their poems. For a workshop to be successful, all participants need to give helpful, honest comments, being sensitive to the writer's feelings. Workshops are a great way to improve and learn new things about your own poetry.

7. **Activity: Write a letter to a poet.** Many libraries have sources in their reference sections that help people get in touch with poets. *The Directory of American Poets and Fiction Writers* and *Writers for Young Adults* are two sources that provide addresses and other pertinent information on contemporary poets. Make a poet's day by writing him or her a letter explaining why a poem means so much to you.

8. **Recommended Resources: Books.** If you've ever wondered about behind-the-scenes information on a poem, there are two good sources edited by Paul B. Janeczko to check out. *The Place My Words Are Looking For* is a book for younger readers that contains poems and the poets' explanation of their ideas and writing processes. *Poetspeak* also presents poems and commentary by the poets for more advanced readers.

9. **Recommended Resources: Museums.** To learn more about Emily Dickinson's life and work, you can visit her home in Amherst, Massachusetts. Seeing the place where she wrote many of her poems can give you a greater insight to her work. Find out more about the Emily Dickinson Museum at its Web site: http://www.emilydickinsonmuseum.org.

GLOSSARY

blank verse: unrhymed iambic pentameter, a special meter formed by repeating five iambs (bum-BUM) in a row

colloquialisms: informal words used in casual conversation

confessional: of a literary movement from the 1940s through the 1960s that encouraged the exploration of personal insights and emotions

contemporary: of the present time

Cubist: of Cubism, a visual arts movement that emphasized breaking objects down into shapes to get a better understanding of their form

Harlem Renaissance: an artistic movement in the early 1900s that celebrated African-American literature, visual art, drama, and music

Imagist: of Imagism, a literary movement in the early 1900s that emphasized the importance of images

meters: patterns of rhythms (accented syllables) in a line or entire poem

narrative poems: poems that tell a story

oral tradition: the practice of passing on information through the spoken word

rhyme scheme: the pattern of rhymes

rhymes: words that echo one another because of their similar sounds

Romantic Movement: a movement in the arts from the late 1700s to mid-1800s in Europe that celebrated individual beliefs, emotions, and nature

slang: colorful words and phrases made popular during certain time periods or within certain groups of people

sonnets: 14-line poems that follow a special form

SELECTED WORKS

Brooks, Gwendolyn. *Selected Poems*. New York: HarperCollins, 1999.

Cummings, E. E. *Selected Poems*. New York: Liveright Publishing, 1994.

Dickinson, Emily. *The Collected Poems of Emily Dickinson*. New York: Random House, 1988.

Hughes, Langston. *The Collected Poems of Langston Hughes*. New York: Knopf, 1995.

Keats, John. *Selected Poems*. New York: Penguin Classics, 2000.

McClatchy, J. D., ed. *The Vintage Book of Contemporary American Poetry*. New York: Vintage, 2003.

Plath, Sylvia. *The Collected Poems*. New York: HarperCollins, 1981.

Shakespeare, William. *A Treasury of Shakespeare's Verse*. New York: Houghton Mifflin, 2000.

Whitman, Walt. *Leaves of Grass (Modern Library Series)*. New York: Random House, 1993.

Williams, William Carlos. *Selected Poems*. New York: New Directions, 1985.

INDEX